This Strange

Quantum World

& You

"Patricia Topp's book offers a bridge between the world of form and matter's true essence. Easy to read, it offers a straightforward understanding in an area of previous wonder. Having been an educator for over two decades, I plan to use this book and its experiments with my 4th grade class. This is a must-read for any age!"

—Laurel Petersen

"After reading This Strange Quantum World & You, I understood a lot more about science than I used to. The drawings and experiments help to give a more clear idea of what's being explained. This book makes reading about a tough subject fun and easy to understand."

—Natalie Nix, 7th grade student, Roseville Jr. High

"This book flows from science to the beyond. Quality, thoughtful reading for children from eleven to one hundred and eleven."

—Terry Turk, M.S., M.A., L.P.C.

This Strange Quantum World & You

PATRICIA TOPP

BLUE DOLPHIN

Published by Blue Dolphin Publishing, Inc.
P.O. Box 8, Nevada City, CA 95959
Web : www.bluedolphinpublishing.com
Orders: 1-800-643-0765

ISBN: 1-57733-035-8

Library of Congress Cataloging-in-Publication Data

Topp, Patricia, 1923–
    This strange quantum world & you / Patricia Topp.
        p.   cm.
    Summary: Explains how scientists discovered the different
qualities of the smaller-than-an-atom world, including particles
and waves, ripple patterns, interference patterns, and the theory
that the universe is the most powerful Bose-Einstein condensate.
    ISBN 1-57733-035-8
    1. Science—Juvenile literature.   [1. Physics.]   I. Title.
Q163.T66 1998
539.7—dc21   98-30955
                                                               CIP
                                                                AQ

Cover design: Lito Castro
Illustrations: R.L. Crabb

First printing, July 1999

Printed in the United States of America

10   9   8   7   6   5   4   3   2   1

For the kids from nine to ninety
who want to know more about
how their world works.

From a science test given to eleven-year-olds:

"When they broke open molecules,
they found they were only stuffed with atoms.
But when they broke open atoms,
they found them stuffed with explosions."

Table of Contents

This Strange

Quantum World

& You

1

The Atomic Age Begins with a Bang

More than two thousand years ago the Greeks talked of the universe as being made of tiny marble-like things, which they called **atoms.** For many years this seemed to be a useful way to view the world.

Then, scientists of the 1800s began to change their thinking about atoms being solid. They thought that each atom must be more like a small solar system with a center like a little sun. They called this center the **nucleus.** They thought even smaller **particles** circled, like planets on their paths around this sun. They called these tiny specks **electrons.** Like our solar system, the atoms were made mostly of great spaces.

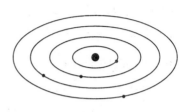

Their parts were thought to be held together by a force like the one you can feel when you put the south and north poles of two magnets close together.

The scientists believed that they could find out how most things in the world worked if they could study these atoms. No one knew whether the scientists were right or wrong about this. Even after the first microscopes were invented, the atoms proved to be too small to see.

Is it crazy to believe in a world that you cannot see? Many scientists did not think so. In the early 1900s, they made many discoveries even in the smaller-than-an-atom world.

And then along came Professor Einstein! He did not use a microscope. He just put on his thinking cap and came up with all sorts of strange ideas about energy and the solid stuff of the universe, which is called **mass** or **matter.**

Einstein thought that matter could be changed into energy. This idea was expressed in his now famous rule, $E = mc^2$. This meant that if you take the speed of light (c), multiply it by itself, and multiply again by some mass (m) of stuff, you would get energy (E). **Energy in a big way!**

Multiplying by the speed of light will get you a **big** number. Light was thought to be the fastest thing in the universe. It speeds along at 186,000 miles (or 300,000 km) per second. That would be fast enough to shoot a rocket ship more than seven times around Earth in one second!

Scientists working with Professor Einstein's rule did find that great amounts of energy were set free even when they exploded very small amounts of matter. **They found that atoms could be split right apart, making even smaller parts.** Two atomic bombs made by using Einstein's rule were used during World War II to destroy two very large cities. With these two blasts the world entered the Atomic Age.

2

Discoveries About Light in the 1800s

In order to understand why Professor Einstein worked with the speed of light to unlock the secrets of this smaller-than-an-atom world, it is necessary to know a few facts about light.

Sunlight is a form of **radiant** energy (coming from rays). The sun and other stars burn with constant explosions something like those of atomic bombs. These explosions send out waves of light. These waves act like the waves of the ocean. Small waves follow one another quickly. Longs waves come less often.

You can try this experiment to see how waves behave:

Tie a long jump rope to a tree. Take the other end of the rope and shake (**vibrate**) it gently up and down. The long waves will pass down the rope looking like this:

Short waves will pass looking like this:

Notice it was the energy that moved down the rope. The rope stayed where it was. Waves pass through things without taking them along.

For many thousands of years people have known that the heat and light from the sun were what made it possible to live on Earth. Many people of long ago worshiped the sun as a god. They told wonderful stories about what made the sun travel across the sky. Yet until the last few hundred years, very little was known about the sun and its light.

In the 1600s, people began to study their surroundings in a more scientific way. While studying the rays from the sun, one scientist discovered that the light from the sun could be broken up into the colors of the rainbow. He found that light rays would bend when they passed through a three-sided piece of glass or when they passed through water. You can try one of these experiments to see this for yourself:

Place a **prism** (a glass shaped in a long triangle) or a piece of cut glass in a sunny window. When the angle is right, a rainbow will appear on the opposite wall. This rainbow is called the **color spectrum.**

If you do not have a piece of glass to use, you can bend light rays using water. Fill a shallow pan with water. At one end place a pocket mirror. Angle it so that the sun shines through a window onto the mirror. The water will bend the light rays and separate them. You will see a rainbow on the wall or on the ceiling of the room.

When we speak of light, we are usually talking about light that we can see, but not always. Our brain tells our eyes to see the long waves of light as the color red. As the waves grow shorter, we see the colors in the order of the rainbow. The shortest rays we can see are blue-violet. But this visible light is only a small part of the story. **Most light is light which we cannot see.**

In the 1800s, a scientist checking the color spectrum (rainbow) with a thermometer found that the rays gave off differing amounts of heat. The blue-violet rays were the coolest. The red rays were the hottest. Then he found something really surprising. When he moved the thermometer beyond the band of red light, the temperature on the thermometer went still higher. He had discovered invisible heat waves. These rays were named **infrared** rays.

Soon another scientist found that there was also something unusual at the other end of the rainbow. The rays there could cause chemical changes. These rays were named **ultraviolet** rays. If you have ever had a painful sunburn, you have experienced ultraviolet rays.

X-rays were discovered next, and then the race was on to find other kinds of radiation. One discovery followed another. By the late 1800s, enough was known so that one scientist could put the puzzle of the light rays together. He said that all the rays moved like electricity and magnetism. He called the range of radiation the **electromagnetic spectrum.** Like the color spectrum, the kind of ray depended upon the length of its waves.

You can see that visible light was just a small part of this range of light rays. Cosmic rays are the shortest. Many trillions of vibrations of cosmic waves might measure less than an inch. It would not be possible for you to vibrate your jump rope wave-maker **that** fast. One of the longest waves of the spectrum might stretch clear across Texas.

cosmic rays

gamma rays

x-rays

ultraviolet

visible light

infrared

radio waves

electric waves

3

What Is This Strange Quantum World?

The next puzzle for the scientists was to find out just what these light rays were. The answers were so surprising that many scientists could not believe what their arithmetic was telling them. They found that the rules of the universe which worked for things big enough to see could not be used to understand light and the small parts that made up each atom. They felt as though someone had pulled the rug out from under their feet. You know how it feels when you are playing a game, and someone changes the rules!

The scientists discovered that all light rays always traveled at the same speed. But even though the light seemed to travel in waves, the waves sometimes acted as if they were made out of particles. The particles were not specks of stuff. They were so small that they were more like locations than like things. Single ones were named **photons.** These photons did not travel to Earth separately, however. They came in little packets of photons which Professor Einstein called **quanta.** (You can think of this word as meaning a quantity of something.) Because Professor Einstein had spoken of photons as quanta, this new science was called **quantum theory.** (A theory is the scientists' best guess at the time.)

Scientists working with a beam that could shoot out these photons one at a time found that they acted strangely. By the time they had crossed the room, they had started to stick to one another. That is why Professor Einstein had found light traveling in little packets. Scientists called the kind of energy which bound the packets **bosons.** You can think of them as particles of crazy glue. They form relationships, (sticky stuff that fits things together). Scientists think that there are two classes of things which make up the universe. Bosons are one class. You will read about the other class later in the book.

To investigate this quantum world, the scientists built huge (miles around) atom smashers. In them the atoms were speeded up and made to crash into one another, so that they would split. The scientists still could not see the atoms, nor the little particles caused by the collisions. But they could study the tracks that were made on a photographic plate as they flew by. This was like learning about an animal by studying its tracks.

By doing these crash tests the scientists found that atoms could be broken down into smaller and smaller pieces. More than two hundred of these smaller-than-an-atom pieces have been found. And more are possible.

New names were needed for all these little particles. The scientists invented some very strange names. If you like to play with words, you can have fun with their names like this:

"Listen you **boson,** your **atom**obile crashed into my **atom**obile. You **omega me-son** dollars. Don't **lambda** out of here until you put your **alpha-beta** to work. Put your **sigma**ture on this paper. Don't **quark** at me. It was your fault."

4

Particles/Waves

Things in this quantum world acted every bit as strangely as the new names seemed to suggest. In our ordinary world, when we think of particles, we think of solid stuff that might look like these dots. . . . When we think of waves, we expect them to look like the waves you made with your jump rope wave-maker.

But something was different about the electrons spinning in orbits in the atoms. They did not travel in a set orbit like the path Earth takes around the sun. They seemed to travel in unusual ways, sort of like the pattern a tightly stretched string makes when you twang it.

And something else was very different.
**The electrons did not always act like par-
ticles. They could also act like waves of
energy.** The form they took depended upon
which experiment the scientists used to study
them. The scientists could no longer stand
outside of their world and study it. **Their
choice of what method they would use to
study matter and energy made them a part
of their experiments.**

The oddness of this smaller-than-an-atom
world kept amazing the scientists. Just like
you, they were used to how things acted in
the world where things were big enough to
see. If you place a penny on a table, you can
be fairly certain of where it is. And you can
expect that it will be there until someone
moves it.

When the scientists looked for pieces of
atoms, they found that they could only guess

about where they might appear and when they might be there, or on the wave to somewhere else. It would be as if there were appearing and disappearing pennies on the table, and you never could know where to look for the special one you had placed there.

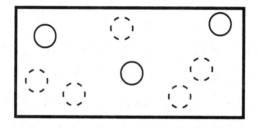

The scientists found that they could only study the changes in a large number of atomic happenings and set odds (make a good guess) on what might happen and when. This would be like setting odds on a horse to win a race. Or it would be like averaging bowling scores to tell how a bowler is likely to score in future games. You could never be sure whether, or when, the bowler might bowl that average number exactly. **In this quantum world, the particles seemed not to be solid. They**

seemed to be only moving locations on waves of energy.

You might want to try seeing it this way. Suppose your class of thirty people were to have a test. Suppose that when the papers were returned, two people had failed, four had D's, twelve had C's, eight had B's, and the rest had passed with flying colors. If your arithmetic teacher then gave you the job of showing this on a bar graph, you would show it some-thing like this.

A B C D E

Now notice that a line drawn along the top of the bars of your graph would look like a wave.

Your graph showed that in your classroom more people were likely to get C's than any other grade. Now if you think of this as a graph about atoms, it would mean that an electron would be more likely to be found on the C part of the wave.

Particle/waves are not like the waves on the sea. What scientists mean when they say that the particles are also waves is that **they are mathematical waves.** They are waves that show the scientists where they are most likely to find the particle they are seeking.

If your class took another test next month, the wave would possibly look about the same, but would probably be slightly different. The quantum world is like that, too. It is a world of **possibly and probably.** Guessing what is, or what will be, in this smaller-than-an-atom world is even chancier that predicting the weather.

The scientists had always thought that they could find the smallest bit of stuff out of which everything else was made. What they discovered in the quantum world was a field of dancing energy.

Think back to the **"atom**obile crash" you read about earlier in this book. Two atoms crashed sending out little pieces of themselves. But something else can happen in the quantum world when two little bits of matter crash. They usually break into pieces. **But magically they may still be the same as they were before, and more pieces of matter may have been created!**

To explain this, you have to remember that quantum stuff is really energy. Atoms go speeding so fast in an atom smasher that they pick up **kinetic** energy. Kinetic energy is the energy of motion. You know that a baseball will not break a pane of glass all by itself. But if you add kinetic energy by throwing the ball. . . .

CRASH!

Suppose that the car crashes in our everyday world could lead to new automobiles being created. That would *really* give headaches to the auto makers.

The scientists found out that they could never find the smallest bits of stuff in this strange quantum world. They found nothing but energy. Does this make you wonder how things in your world seem so solid?

5

What Is Solid?

If you know now that matter and energy are pretty much the same, you may be wondering why that penny which you placed on the table did not go right through it. Something strange must be going on. You can get a little understanding about this by trying the following experiment:

String a large four-hole button on a long loop of string as shown in the picture. Hold the ends of the loop and twirl the button, so that the string twists. Then pull the ends of the loop outward, so that the string untwists. The flat button will look like a ball. Have someone else spin the button for you. Now **very lightly** touch the button. It will hit your fingers again and again. If you could spin it fast enough, it would feel like a solid ball.

You are familiar with another thing that tricks your senses like this. In moving pictures, each reel of film is made up of many little still pictures. When the pictures are run fast enough past the light, you can watch the scenes move and change.

When the atoms in our universe are spinning fast, they fool our senses. They seem to us to be solid. But the answer to the question, "What is solid?" is that—**nothing is solid! Everything is energy spinning at great rates of speed.**

The particles that make up seemingly solid things are held together very tightly.

When quantum particles are kept tightly in small places, they speed up. The tighter the space, the faster they spin. The nucleus (the "sun" of each atom) spins almost as fast as the speed of light. Think of a rock and, in your mind's eye, see it boiling with energy. Now hold your hand in front of your eyes. Can you think of it as being made of dancing energy?

You have read that bosons are one class of the two basic classes which make up the universe. You may be wondering what the other class is. It is called the class of **fermions.** These are the energies that the bosons stick together to make up everything that seems to us to be solid.

When the atomic bombs went off, mass was exploded into energy. But suppose you were to reverse Professor Einstein's rule. If you divided the speed of light out of all that energy, you would have some matter back again. This is what happens when light rays come to Earth. They are absorbed or bounced off something, and can be transformed into matter. The plant kingdom is always busy changing light into the food you eat. Your body changes the food into you. This is not nearly so exciting as an atomic blast. But if it were not possible, there would be no you.

All the solid seeming things of the universe are made of energy.

6

Information Networks

As we have seen, it is the nature of all things to vibrate, to make waves. You cannot see the atoms of a tree or a rock moving back and forth, but you can be sure that they are doing so. All the atoms of your body are vibrating, too.

In the 1960s, the young people invented the sayings "bad vibes" and "good vibes." They meant that they could feel the waves of energy coming from others. You know how easy it is for your mother to know when you are angry even if you do not say or do anything. You are sending out waves of unhappy energy, and she is feeling them. If you are

good at sensing energies, you will be able to feel the soothing waves she sends back to you.

Mother Nature usually sends out "good vibes." Do you remember how good it feels when you walk along a beach or through the woods?

You can do the following experiment to show yourself how vibrations can carry messages:

Find two paper cups. Punch holes in the bottoms of the cups. Find a cord about three times as long as you are tall. Take an old candle and wax the cord. Thread the cord through the bottom of each cup. Fasten it inside with knots, or by threading the ends through two buttons. Ask a friend to stretch the cord and put an ear to the open end of one cup. You talk into the open end of the other cup. The vibrations will pass from your voice through the cord to your friend's ear.

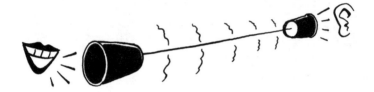

All things in the universe seem to be connected in a network of information carried on vibrations.

If you have watched a spider on its web (network), you may have seen how it acted when

an insect landed on the web. As the insect lands, the spider feels the vibrations of its web. This is information about just where on the web dinner is waiting.

Another time you would find a network of information would be when using your computer. Computers use (electromagnetic) vibrations to connect you with information from all around the world. Information links everyone who is connected to the Internet with everyone else on the net out there in **cyberspace.** Messages flash clear around the globe in the blink of an eye.

We do not usually think of our bodies as being networks of information, yet they are. If your brain tells you, "Heads up, a ball is coming," your body knows what to do. When your brain signals thirst, you go to the water tap. Hunger takes you to the kitchen. Your body knows how to act right away if some germs enter it. We are so used to our bodies serving us in this way that we do not think about it. But if your arm or leg would not move when you gave it the signal to do so, you would want to know why the information was not getting through to your muscles.

The networks of information that you have read about in this chapter are connections in which the signals do **not** travel faster than the speed of light. Even though light is very speedy, these appear to be local connections. They are connections in just your neighborhood of the universe. **But some events in this quantum universe can happen faster than the speed of light.**

7

Now You See It; Now You Don't

In order to live our lives well, we want to know what happened any time something goes wrong. We want to know the cause. Sometimes this is not possible, but many times it is. The quantum world is much more mysterious. There are connections which allow events very, very far from one another in space to act upon one another **faster** than the speed of light.

Electrons in atoms seem to be able to jump from one orbit to another without traveling between them. They seem to be

able to exist here and then exist there with no time to get from here to there. It is as if Earth could suddenly disappear and pop up being Pluto.

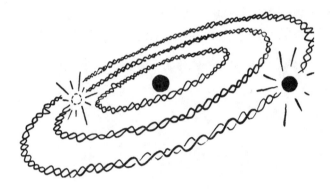

An electron which makes this sort of "quantum leap" seems to be everywhere and nowhere all at once. It has a way of smearing out into all possible orbits before making its leap. A magician would feel right at home in this quantum world. It is a **now you see it; now you don't** kind of place. Related events can happen exactly at once, even if they do not seem to have any connection. In some way, each event is acted upon by the whole universe. The causes of the events are spread all through the information network of the whole universe. So that what causes one atom to fly apart or another to form is well hidden from the scientists.

The scientists have found that our minds work in much the same way. Information is held all through our brains. You can make quantum leaps with your thoughts. If your body could do this, you could skate, play ball, and go bike riding, all at the same time, while you were deciding how you wanted to spend your day.

8

Caught in the Web

It is the odd actions of light which help explain the way the universe works. The scientists do not know the causes for the happenings in the quantum world. They do have some ideas about what does happen.

In one test the scientists sent a beam of photons toward a screen. The screen had two slits which would let the photons of light through. The scientists put the things they needed to test for **particles** on the other side of the screen. When the beam of photons came to the screen, it chose only one slit to move through.

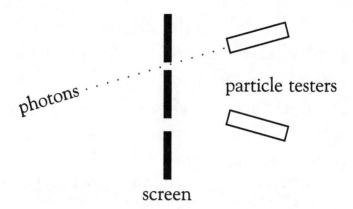

particle testers

screen

In a second test, the scientists used material behind the screen to test for **waves**. As before, they sent a beam of photons toward the screen. The photons passed through both slits at once. **This time the photons acted like waves!**

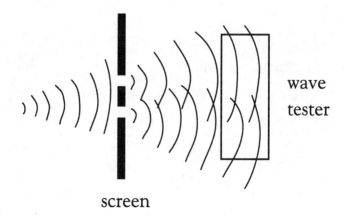

wave tester

screen

Do you see why the scientists were puzzled? They wondered how the photons "knew" what they were being tested for. The photons seemed to be conscious (aware) in some way. The scientists' thoughts seemed to have made them a part of their own experiments. They were caught in the information web of the universe. **And so are you!**

Look at the second test picture again. Do you see that the waves crossed over one another? They interfered with one another to make a pattern. The scientists named this an **interference pattern.** You can try the following experiment to show yourself how this works:

Fill a large shallow pan with water. Drop two pennies in opposite corners. If you look very quickly, you will see a pattern of ripples on the surface of the water. You have made an interference pattern which lasted just a short time.

There are two modern inventions which may help you to have some understanding of how nature uses interference patterns. One is the **laser light**, and the other is **holography.**

Most lamps scatter light rays in the same way that you and your friends scatter when running around on the playground at recess. In laser lights, the rays all march in step like soldiers on parade. The beam is very strong because it is very focused. There are many uses for these lasers. Doctors can use them in operations. Factory workers can cut metal with them. Photographers with the right gear can use them to make holograms. These are three-dimensional pictures. They have length, width, and depth.

The figure below shows how it works. A laser light is shone through a sort of "magic mirror." Half of the light goes right through the magic mirror, bounces off a real mirror, then focuses a ball. Half of the light reflects from the magic mirror, bounces off two more mirrors, and focuses on the ball. The beams interfere with one another like the ripples that you saw in your water experiment.

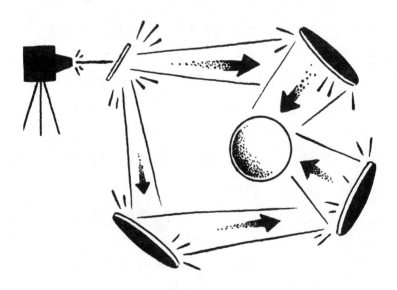

The camera makes a photographic plate of this ripple pattern. It stores the pattern, and when another laser light is shone through the photo plate, the 3-D ball hangs out in space looking real.

Very interesting! But the best is yet to come.

You know that when you tear a regular snapshot into pieces, each piece will show only a part of the picture. But if a photographer drops a holographic plate and breaks it, a very strange thing happens. **A laser beam shone through any single piece of the photo plate will show the whole picture, no matter which piece the photographer chooses to try.** Each piece will not give as clear a picture as the whole, but nothing will be missing. The information of the hologram seems to be spread everywhere within it. This is like what happens when an electron takes a quantum leap and seems to be everywhere at once.

There are ways in which our universe is using this 3-D interference pattern storage system of information. The patterns are not stored in water, as in your experiment. They are not stored in photo plates, as in holography. They are stored in something much more mysterious. You will read about this in the next chapters of the book.

9

Faster Than the Speed of Light

By Professor Einstein's time in the early 1900s, much was known about light. But there were still puzzles. Scientists knew that sound waves had to have something to travel through. We hear sound waves which travel through the air. The cries of whales are heard through water. If you bang on a metal pipe, the pipe will carry the sound. But what was carrying the light waves through empty space to Earth?

Perhaps space was not really empty. The scientists began to think of space as what they called a **force field.** You can get some sort of understanding of this by trying this experiment using a magnet and iron filings. This will show you a magnetic field in two dimensions on a flat surface.

💡 Put a magnet under a sheet of paper. Sprinkle iron filings (or crumble pieces of steel wool) on top of the paper. You will notice that the little pieces are forced to fall in a certain pattern. You cannot see nor feel what is pulling them into that pattern, but the iron filings can feel it. The magnetic force field decides their pattern.

The scientists knew that whatever carries light had to be able to take it everywhere in three dimensions. Imagine a deep pan full of water. It would have three dimensions. If you stirred it, ripples would appear everywhere within it, not just on the surface as they did when you dropped the pennies in shallow water. A ripple pattern in 3-D would be formed, and remember this, **ripple patterns carry information.**

The water acted like a field of information. In your experiment with the iron filings, the field of information was a magnetic field. In somewhat the same way, light waves and information are carried by an energy field in space which the scientists call the **quantum vacuum.** (But this does not mean that they think that space is empty like a vacuum.) **The quantum vacuum is thought to contain every possibility within it.** The scientists cannot tell what causes this mysterious force field to be there and to be able to carry information. But they can tell a good deal about how it works.

The scientists think that this force field is made of bosons. The field carries the information to tell the bosons how to stick the fermions together to make all the seemingly solid things of our universe. Atoms and **molecules** (combined atoms) have north and south poles. The bosons can line them up like soldiers on parade with all the north poles facing the same way. Then the bosons can "crazy glue" them in place.

You can try the following experiment that will give you a little understanding of how this works:

💡 You will need a magnet, a large nail, and a pin. First try to pick up the pin using only the nail. You will see that this cannot be done. Now take to nail in one hand with the point away from you. Stroke one end of the magnet down the nail. Keep stroking only one way. Do not stroke toward yourself. Do this for a few minutes. Then set the magnet aside. Now you can use the nail as a

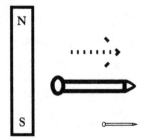

magnet to pick up the pin. Your stroking on the nail with the magnet has made its atoms line up in a more orderly way. You have made a (not very strong) Bose-Einstein condensate.

Scientists call things which are very orderly **Bose-Einstein condensates.** This is not as hard to understand as it sounds. Bose and Einstein were important scientists whose names are honored by using them to name things which act like magnets and lasers. Condensate does *not* mean anything like thick canned milk. It means acting in an orderly way.

What happens in a Bose-Einstein condensate is that all the separate atoms stop acting separately. But they do not just **act** together. **They really become just one whole thing.**

You have read that the quantum leap electron could spread itself everywhere. You have read about how in the information of the hologram was held everywhere within it.

In a like way, the scientists think that **every point in the quantum universe touches every other point. Nothing can be separate.** The scientists believe that this is so because the universe is the most powerful Bose-Einstein condensate. It is the largest and most orderly information network.

In this powerful force field are some connections which act faster than those which are made by light traveling through your neighborhood of the universe. They are connections which are **not** local. They can cause related events, no matter how far apart, to happen without one seeming to cause the other. They happen like quantum leaps.

Do you remember reading how the photons in the scientists' experiments seemed to "know" in some way what they were being tested for? The photon beams and the scientists seemed somehow connected. Well, they really were. **In this strange quantum world everything is connected. Messages can** travel faster than the speed of light because they somehow travel in thoughts.

We are, each and every one of us, woven into a great 3-D web of vibrating energies. We are within it, and it is within us. **The most unusual thing about this web of energy is that it seems to be conscious like we are. It is able to exchange information within all its parts like we do within our bodies.**

10

What's It to You?

Our lives have been changed forever by the discoveries in the smaller-than-an-atom world. The power of the atomic bomb blasts shocked the world. Scientists began to look for peaceful ways to use their discoveries. Their discoveries are being used to send astronauts out to explore space. They are being used to make a network of instant communications around the world. They are being used in industry and in healing. And think how different your world would be if you had no television or computer.

Understanding about this strange quantum world may be even more important in another way. Some scientists believe that we are conscious because our minds act like Bose-Einstein condensates. Our senses send messages from our bodies and from our surroundings to our brains. Our brains put the messages together into some sort of way which makes sense to us. For each of us this forms our picture of our world.

Sometimes we each feel ourselves to be separate from everyone and everything else. Have you believed that you could get away with doing something sneaky because nobody except you was watching? Have you ever wondered who is listening when you pray or say grace at table? Just who is watching or listening? **The answer is that you are watching and listening. And you are not separate from the universe.**

The particle part of you feels itself to be separate. (I am me. I am not you.) But there is also a wave part of you. (This is a part of you which most people cannot see.) It is the electromagnetic part within you and around your body. This is the part which can send out those angry or soothing "vibes." It is the part of you which connects you to your family, to your country, to your Earth, and to all the universe.

You are like a broken bit of a holographic plate of the universe. You cannot be really clear about the whole picture. But nothing is missing from you. We are each our own part and the whole. That is why each and every one of us is important.

In this strange quantum world you are connected even with the stars. The waves of your thoughts reach out in ways you can imagine and in ways too strange to imagine. **So you must be careful about what you create with your thoughts.**

The scientists who made the atomic bombs have had more than fifty years to wish they had not thought to make bombs. For more than half a century all the large cities of

North American and Europe have been in great danger. They could have been flattened by atomic bombs within minutes. The scientists learned that having more power meant that they had to be more careful about their thoughts.

How would you think differently if you really believed that what you think could change the world in some way?

* * * * * *

To the scientists, the quantum picture of the universe seemed to be a new idea. Yet for centuries people all lands have thought of each smallest rock or plant or animal as being aware. And they have used the idea of the net or web to tell this very same story. The American Indians told it like this:

"Grandmother Spider was sad because the people of Earth were not aware of their connection with nature, the heavens, and holy order. Leaping from the earth to the sky and back to the earth, over and over again, she spun her giant web. Wherever the strands of her web crossed, a new star was born in the heavens. When she had finished, the sky was full of stars and humans could see that they, the Earth, the heavens, the gods, fate, and purpose were all linked together."

(This story was paraphrased from the material of Kathleen Burt.)

The story which has been told in *This Strange Quantum World and You* is the scientists' best guess at the time. There is more than one guess about how the universe works. There will be more discoveries about this in your lifetime.

Stay tuned!

PATRICIA TOPP, a resident of Michigan, received an M.A. in Education from Wayne State University and was a grade school teacher for 32 years, as well as a tutor for adult illiterates. Continuing to develop her skills after retirement, she has also written *Stepping Off Life's Sad Merry-Go-Round: Metaphorically Speaking,* as well as numerous articles and poetry. As a counselor, she is certified in Clinical Hypnotherapy, Imperative Self-Analysis, and Neuro-Linguistic Programming.